T0171352

A Tribute to My Wife, "Rutha M. Hall" with "3" Little Angels God Sent

LARRY D. HALL

authorHOUSE®

AuthorHouse™
1663 Liberty Drive
Bloomington, IN 47403
www.authorhouse.com
Phone: 1 (800) 839-8640

Published by AuthorHouse 02/07/2019

ISBN: 978-1-5462-7894-8 (sc)
ISBN: 978-1-5462-7895-5 (hc)
ISBN: 978-1-5462-7893-1 (e)

Library of Congress Control Number: 2019901426

Print information available on the last page.

This book is printed on acid-free paper.

Contents

Introdction ..ix
I. Meeting and marriage. ... 1
II. First Seperation. .. 7
III. Trying to make a new start. ... 12
IV. Our first home at 6616 south Peoria17
V. Life at our old/new address 6608 south Peoria, for the
 2nd time. ... 24
VI. Moving to our new home at 9304 south Vanderpoel. 28
VII. Little angel # 1, "Akria Brooks".39
VIII. Little angel 2, "Aaliyah Brooks" better know as "Le-Le".45
IX. Little angel "3", "Amelia Brooks" better know as "Fat-Fat".49
X. Three little angels, coming together.53
XI. Where it all begin "6608 south Peoria", 3rd floor.59

Introduction

THIS TRIBUTE IS TO the 'woman' that before her, I was less than 'nothing', with her, I started to become 'something', and now I'm 'invicible'. She brought me from nothing, to something, too someone who can change the world.

When I was a boy growing up, most people said, "I wouldn't live to reach manhood, if I did, I would end up in jail", but by the grace of 'God' and the support from my wife, I prove them all wrong.

I give thanks everyday to 'God' for putting you in my life. I also give thanks to you for staying with me after all the wrong, pain, disappointment, and suffering I cause you. But most of all, for not killing me in my sleep (God know's you had every reason to do so).

You have been the anchor that kept my ship from dripping away, the thing that held it in place when it was driffing out to the open sea. Because of you I was able to charter a new course, maintain it, and reach our goals.

If 'God' had not put you in my life, my ship would have sail to places unknown. A place were there is no future (where time stands still), a place where lost people end up (hell on earth).

Thank you for saving me from that, (thank you for showing me the right directions), to the right places in life, and a (special thank's) too you, for helping me get there.

I can't even see life (without you with me) all I can see without you 'is' a empty space. That seems like a black hole with no light at the end (a dead end). My future would be nothing without you being in the future with me. You are my better half. That part of me where good exists. The part that will take me from the darkness into the light.

This book is a tribute to you (my wife) Rutha M. Hall because, you are the 'wind' in my sail's where ever my ship end's up, it's because of your 'wind' and 'God's' navigation. I was just the tool he used. A blind man that couldn't see.

So, this book is a tribute to the most wonderful woman, 'God' could ever send a man, he sent me you "Rutha M. Hall". A woman that could stay with a man after all the wrong and bad things I did to you 'thank you' from the bottom of my heart.

You stayed with me after all the disrespect, the women, the drugs, and alcohol for over 30 years, again 'thank you', and "please!!, please!!!" forgive me (once more).

Because I know this (ship) has other goals to reach and I know this (ship) will reach those 'goals' because of your 'wind' and 'God's' navigation, how can it not.

Thank you for being my wife, "Rutha M. Hall" you saved my life.

I. *Meeting and marriage;*

❦

My WIFE'S NAME IS *(Rutha M. Hall), I first met her when I came home from Vietnam for my brother's funeral, his name was (Henry Phillip Hall).*

It was in September of 1971 (the worst days of my life). It's as if something inside of me had just been killed, it left a hollow void of emptiness that felt like a hole in my stomach. I felt sick inside like life was no longer worth living. Why him? I was in Vietnam, it shouldn't been me. My life now felt like a lost soul. I was blind with angry, life had no meaning, why him? This was all I could think about.

I had just lost one of the closet things to my heart (my brother). We were just 10 months apart (even though we fought throughout our childhood), God had brought us very close before I left for Vietnam. We had become each others shallow. We went everywhere together.

Had I been home at the time and not in Vietnam, I would have been in the car wreck. The car wreck that killed my brother. This was very hard for me to understand, why him? And not me. I was where people are killed; he was where people suppose to be safe.

Since God knows everything, (he knew it would be our last time seeing

1

each other) that's why it felt so 'special', when we said goodbye (for the last time). Neither one of us knew at the time, we would never see each other again (in life). Those are the things that only 'God' knows. However God did allow him to leave behind (2) sons, "Greg & Gerry Hall" they would become like my sons also.

The news of my brother's death had turned my world upside down. I needed someone or something to make me smile again. The funeral was in Mississippi, my father "Henry F. Hall" had come from Chicago to attend the funeral. After the funeral I went back to Chicago with him. I just couldn't stay in Mississippi with my brother gone. His death cause a deep scar inside me that would take along time to heal.

My step mother Annette Hall, "told me about her play daughter" and wanted me to meet her. Being the dog I still was, this was right down my alley. This could be just what the doctor ordered (putting a dog on another sent).

The party was on a saturday even, my step mother had given it so that I could meet her play daughter. I loved parties that meant women and drinking (still something that existed inside). That made me stop feeling sorry for myself and start thinking about the party.

My father and I went to pick her up (I nerver saw her before) so I had know way of knowing what to look for. She could have been big as a house or ugly as sin, I didn't know.

When we got there (2 young ladies came out). I didn't know 'who' was 'who', both were nice looking lady's. They both had lovely faces and pretty smiles. I was happy for that.

Although one was kind of on the fat side but looked very nice (pleasantly plump), the other one was very well built, and very nice looking to boot. I was hoping (her play daughter), was the well built one with the pretty smile (she was).

When we got back for the party, some friends of mine were there from the west side. One of my friend's was making eyes at my step mother's play daughter (I step up quickly to let him know she was spoken for). In fact, we spent the whole party with each other. The even went so fast.

When the party was over (late night) time to go, I didn't want to say good night. I called a cab to take her home, then rode in the cab with her home, and then had to ride in the cab back home. There was something about this young

lady different from the others, it was hard for me to say good night. I could feel it when I first saw her.

This feeling cost me double because I didn't want to say good night. It was something about her (maybe cause I hadn't had sex with her before) but it was more than that. She had a special goodness in her that made everyone around her feel good. This was something at the time, I didn't have. I made everyone around me feel bad. Because only people like me, loved being around people like me (bad people).

Because at the time (I consider myself) a player, and lady's man. God's gift to women. So, why was this woman controlling my thoughts.

I couldn't get her off my mind. I couldn't want for Sunday to come (it was Saturday then), I had to see her now!!. We spent that Sunday even together, we went to a movie that night (X rated). I couldn't wait to get her home with me, we had just seen foreplay, and now it was time too play.

That night was like magic, with all the lights, and exploring of fulfillment (all pile up in one). That night seal the deal (God put us together), this was his plan. I thought it was me but now I know it was him. Because God knows our past and our future. Thank you 'God'.

All through the years we were married, I did all I could do to spoil God's plan but we can't spoil God's plan. No matter how hard we try, we can't spoil his plan, because (God's plan) is made in stone that can't be broken.

After spending the whole week together, it was now time for me to return to Vietnam. I had been home for 2 weeks for my brother's funeral. I had to go back to Vietnam after that. This wonderful lady had almost erased the pain of my brother's death and the thought of the war I was returning to in Vietnam. She was what the doctor ordered.

When it came time to say goodbye, it was 'so, so' very hard to do but when the army call's, you have too come. So, I had to say goodbye and go back to Vietnam.

After returning, I had about 4 months remaining in Vietnam. I could return back to the states after that. Those 4 months were longer than the 8 months I had already served. I almost lost my life during those 4 months. But God wouldn't allow another son to be taken, at that time. When the 4 months were over, I returned back to the states, Fort Orr Washington.

This was part of God's plan, because when I reach the airport, I was

going to take the first flight down south or Chicago. The first flight leaving was for Chicago.

It was in late January 1972, I had just left a warm place and now returning to Chicago (in full winter). I almost froze to death before I made it home. I made the mistake of throwing my army clothes away at the airport and dressing in civilians clothes (in the winter), this was a bad idea. I almost froze to death, trying to be cool. I had to take a cab from the airport, too my home at 6616 south Peoria, for a great cost. The price of being cool and almost freezing to death.

The second I got home, I couldn't wait to call (Mae) and tell her, "I'm home". She came home with my step mother that even. That night was like magic once more (we belong together), I felt it again. This was something new to me (these feelings is something I never had before), being a player and all. Love sometimes take us by surprise, it happens when we are not looking.

That's why it was a shock to everyone that knew me and some people that didn't when I ask, "her to marry me", she said, "yes". If she only knew I had a drug problem, the answer may have been "no", thank God she didn't. Since this was God's plan it wouldn't have matter any way. Because he knew we would work it out, God's knows everything.

After saying yes to marrying me (we were married at city hall), my step mother was there for the marriage. After we were married, on the way home form city hall, we had I first fight (about who's on first). My step mother had to be a peace maker in the cab all the way back home.

When we got back home, we had our second fight (about how to cook fish), a fight about nothing again. If this was God's plan, it was getting off to a ruff start.

The night of our wedding, I spent on the west side (getting high), in fact, I spent the whole week end on the west siding (getting high). When I came back home, my father and step mother were both very 'angry ' with me. I didn't care, I was married to them. What they though didn't matter to me.

My wife didn't say anything, 'if' she had, I would have went off on her. I was a self center fool at the time. I use to tell my wife, "I could see something she didn't", but I couldn't (a self center person can only see himself), nothing else. So, what I saw was a (self center asshole that though he was something special).

So, to try and made up, I ask my wife to introduce her girlfriend too my friend from Vietnam. He lived on the west side same as her girlfriend. Then

I took them out to a cub on the west side. While we were out that night, my wife's girlfriend and I was making eye's 'plotting' to get together at a later time. She was there for my friend but I wanted her for me. I always wanted the woman I never had even 'if' she was my wife's friend or my friend's date.

I knew this was my wife's best friend and still I tried to make a play with her (what an asshole), I 'm asking again "Please!!, please!!!" "for give me.

I had just gotten married to the most wounderful woman that 'God' could have given any man on earth and still I couldn't be fateful. I don't deserve a great woman like you. There are no words that I could say that would make that right (except say staying with a asshole like me) thank you.

In spite of that, we did have alot of great times living with my mother and father. On the weekends my father would be gone out drinking. My stepmother would invite the whole family over and we would party hardy until my father came home. The party was over after that. Then, I would go out for the rest of the weekend, partying even harder, staying out all night, and sometimes the whole weekend.

After living with my father on the first floor (for about 6 months), my cousin on the 2ⁿᵈ floor moved. This allow my wife and I to be able to get the apartment they moved from. It was a kitchen-net apartment, with 2 other apartments on the 2ⁿᵈ floor that we all shared the bathroom together.

Things were better living in our own apartment but I was still a (party animal), staying out all night. I was chasing everything that wore a dress (for that again) I ask your 'forgiveness'.

A year later my wife's girlfriend from down south moved in with us for a short period of time. Moving another woman in the house with a (dog) was like leaving a steak out un-guarded. You know a dog will attack a steak, even if it's guarded.

That's just what I tried to do (make a play at her girlfriend), so did my father. He was living on the first floor, trying to tip to the 2ⁿᵈ floor. Like father (like son) 2 dogs trying to get the same steak.

Since your friend was a true friend (nothing happen), 'so' this time, there is nothing to forgive. Trying to be an asshole (didn't allow me become a asshole), this time.

Before, God took my father to 'glory' he forgave him for that. He also 'forgave me', the reason I know, 'is' because I was their (so was my wife) the day he died. I felt his givenesse for both of us.

5

Not only did God for give us for that, he forgave us 'for us'. He cause the slate to be whiped clean between my father and me (only God can do that).

Because of God's plan, my wife was able to see much more (in me). She saw me for what I could be, not what I was now. So, she was the one that could see something I didn't, (me) years from now in the future.

My wife was the one that laid down the foundation that given me something (too build from). I was like a ship without an anchor (sailing all over the place), she became my anchor. Although the sailing down the road is still very ruff but now with the anchor (my wife provided) when the sailing began to get ruff (she can keep the ship steady).

II. *First Seperation*

BEFORE WE GOT MARRIED, *my wife was living with her sister on the west side, "Dot" and her family. After we were married she moved in with me (I was living with my father), asking someone to marry you with no place of your own too take them (bad idea).*

The first 6 months of our marriage, I was drawing unemployment from the army. I was trying to feed a drug problem with unemployment benefits. My wife was working on a real job, she was still giving me extra money (she didn't know it was to buy drugs). If she had known (she probably would have given it to me anyway) that's the kind of person she was.

We were living with my father and stepmother, we couldn't aford a place of our own at the time. Or, maybe we could have, 'if' I wasn't spending all my money on drugs.

My wife nor my father or stepmother knew I was using drugs. If they had known, my father would have kicked me out. Everyone was in the dark (I think my wife knew), she just didn't say anything. During that time I wasn't a good person to talk too. I had women problems, drug problems, and drinking

problems. She had just married a mess, a person that needed alot of help. So our problems was just getting started.

My mother, (Annie J. Hall, Broomfield, Easterling) was still living down south (she was still a Hall at the time). I decided to visit her since I wasn't doing anything with my life but wasting it. This was the start of the first major problem with many more problems to follow.

My mother had been married 3 times (trinty), from the first marriage she got 2 sons (1 decesed the other 1 me), from the second marriage she got 2 daughters (something she alway's want), and from the third marriage she found true love (the thing she wanted the most). Was this not a blessed woman?

My mother was a holy woman (from a holy woman come's a holy man), I'm the only man left from my mother's womb. Someday I may become a holy man or just a good man.

While I was down south, (my wife, stepmother, and father) happen to look in my beloning's, my 'work's 'for using drugs fell out. My secert was now known. My father was beside himside, I know he felt like killing me 'if' I was in his reach. Thank God, I was not.

When I returned from down south, my father demanded that I get a job. My wife, even my friend from Vietnam, and everyone in the house were working (execpt me).

So, I decided to look for a job, I got a job at Wards. It didn't pay much but it was a job. This made my wife, even my father happy. Everything seem to start going fine then, our ship was now sailing on smooth waters again. God's plan had started working.

Then my cousin who own the building, marriage broke up. She was now moving back to her building on the first floor, where my father was living, causing him to move back on the 2ⁿᵈ floor, where we were living, making us have to find somewhere else to live.

The move happen during the X-mas holidays, I had a week off my job. I went down south for the holidays, leaving my wife alone when the move accurred. My wife and my cousin moved in together to share the apartment, I was still down south at the time. When I shouldn't been in Chicago with my wife, helping her move. I was down south partying with other women.

I suppose to have come back in a week, I had only a week off my job, but I was gone for 2 weeks. When I returned to my job, I was fired on the spot.

I had abandant my wife and lost my job, 'all' at the same time. God's plan had just took a bad turn.

Our ship was begining to hit ruff waters again. Through all that (my wife stood by me), she saw something in me that was only visiable to her, and God. No one else not even 'me' could see what they saw.

While I was down south my wife had to move with my cousin to a new address with no help from me (missed another move). I didn't even know where she had moved to. My father had called me down south demanding that I come back, 'now'.

Went I got back from down south (after being fired), I was left with nothing to do. I would get up after my wife left for work everyday (go to liquid store), get a bottle of "Wild Irish Rose" then come back home, 'get drunk' while waiting for my friend who worked at "Unite Parcel" to come by, and then get even higher. This is what happen all day every day for months.

I did this for over 6 months, until I became tried myself. I felt totally lost (a ship without a anchor), sailing on the open sea, a 'driffed'. I had lost all my directions, I didn't know which way to go. My life was now at a stand still (a wreck).

My wife's reason for standing by me, only God, and she could see. Because I did something even dumber after that, I moved back down south, and left her all alone (again). I still ask myself today, why? "Would anyone stand by an asshole like me for all those years".

While I was down south, a friend of my cousin's broken in our apartment and stole everything. My wife was afraid to live there after that (could you blame her), I had left her all alone. During this time she couldn't count on me for anything, I couldn't count on myself, so how could anyone else count on me.

I still don't know why my wife decided to do what she did, knowning the kind of person I was. She must have seen something in 'me' that no one else could see, not even my mother. No way would I come to a person who had left me in a time of need. This took a special woman to come to a man she couldn't count on, leaving her job, her family, and coming to a place she never been to before. To a person that didn't respect himself or anyone else, at the time.

I ask my wife to come down south where I was, knowing I wasn't ready for marriage. Still she left all the family she knew to come to a place where she only knew me (a self center asshole). Even after during that, I treated her with so much disrespect (for that I'm truly sorry), please forgive me.

Their's no words that I could never say that would make up for the pain I cost you. I allowed other women to disrespect you because I disrepected you (please forgive me). I know God's plan don't seem like a plan, now. Because only God and my wife could see is plan, I was still in the dark.

The first time my wife met my mother, it was love at first sight. She had said something that wasn't so nice before she first met her. My mother though my wife was one of those fast Chicago women, like some of the women in the south. But when she saw her, it was a different story.

My mother could see the goodness in her, my wife was like the daughter she never had. They started working at the same place, 'yes' my wife got a job right away. Something the women that had lived in my home town all their lives have not done (found a job).

This made alot of people around speak very highly of her and asking why she married someone like me. Everybody in town knew the kind of person I was, 'so' why would a nice good looking young lady marry me? Like I said, "she saw something they didn't, and I didn't", the future for me.

One day when we were down south, my wife said, "I drove pass her sitting on the side of the road like she was a stranger", I can't remember if I did it or not. I did some many bad and disrespectful things, I can't remember just one.

But, 'if' I did that thing, (I know I did) because I was a total asshole at the time. and keep saying you're sorry become an empty word (if you keep having to saying it). but I'm, 'truly sorry' for however many times I need to say it.

My wife's stay down south didn't last long, she could no longer take the treatment I was putting down. She decided to leave and return back to Chicago. The day she left, my mother called me some ugly names, I never though I would ever hear her say (I can't repeat them), they were that bad. This broke my mother's heart, I didn't even care at the time. I though, I wanted her to leave 'so' I could be free to do what I wanted. Something I was during all the time anyway.

My mother said, "I would never find another woman as good as the one I already had' - 'and if I let her get away, I would be sorry for the rest of my life". Always listen to your mother, because she was right (I would have been). I know that now.

The day my wife left, I brought another woman to my mother's house,

(my mother flipped) she called me and the other woman some very bad names (some names my mother never use before). She said, "don't bring that "B" in my house" after breaking down and crying. This should have open my eyes but it didn't, I just didn't care.

After my wife had left, 'I though' I would be happy but I wasn't. Something was missing in my life, it was her. You don't miss your water until your well run dry (my well had just run dry). I tried to keep going but I couldn't, 'so' I returned back to Chicago (where she was). My wife took me back, what a wonderful woman.

III. *Trying to make a new start.*

❧

WHEN I GOT BACK to Chicago, my wife had moved with her older sister "Lou" and her family. This is where my wife lived when she first came to Chicago, over east. It was where my wife lived before she move with her baby sister "Dot", on the west side where she lived when we got married.

She except me back as 'if' nothing had happen. What a woman (something that I could never do), to be able too forgive the way she did after the way I treated her. For that I'm truly sorry, "please!!, please!!!" forgive me.

After being back for about a week (during nothing), I had to start doing something.

So, I got a job working with my father (construction),which I hated everyday going to work. I felt like I was being punished for something (can you believe that)? A self center asshole thinking he's being punished for something (right).

Still thinking I was a gift to women, I was soon back to my old ways again. Staying out most of the night partying and trying to go to work the next day (it wasn't working out). My mother use to say, "you can't burn the

candle at both ends", I now know what that meant. I had started getting burnt in the middle.

My wife got tried of trying to wake me up in the morning and my father got tried of waiting for me in the morning (another lost job). If this was God's plan it would take alot of work. Because my plans were women and partying but those were not the plans God had for me, and his plans are made in stone (un-breakable stone).

My wife was still standing by me and still in my corner, as I said before, "what a woman", God sent. Only a "God" sent woman could keep this ship on course. It was as if God had given her an impossible task with me (making something out of nothing), but then God don't give impossible tasks even if it seems that way.

After losing my second job, I was back to doing hard drugs again. I had a friend on the west side that was strung out to, he called me saying, "he had some drugs from Vietnam", we had been station together in Vietnam.

The best 'coke' in the world come's from Vietnam. I was there before he hung up the phone.

We were sitting around getting high when something came on the TV saying, "working with your hands not getting your finger nails dirty" that was the job for me. I said, "I'm going to check that out", my friend said, "right", and noded back out.

That was the week-end. So, the first thing that monday morning, I went down town to check it out. It was a school that thaught computer training (I alway's wanted to work with computers) now was my chance.

So, I took the tests and passed with flying colors, I was excepted into the computer training school. This made my wife very happy (I had done something to make her happy), after all the unhappiness I cause "thank you God". I now know it was you.

After getting into computer training school, the ship was sailing steady again. I was now starting something that could become my future. I was getting a benefits check from the VA for going to school, this allowed me to be able too help my wife with bills (something she had being paying by herself before). This made me feel a little better about myself.

After completion of computer training school, I got a Job in computers. The ship was on course for sure now, I was getting a regular pay check. Now I could get my wife some of the thing she wanted (like our own apartment).

I was now working with computers this was something I could like during. This was the first time I had a job I really like. Working with my hands not getting my finger nails dirty. That made my wife very happy (I final started doing something right). Still I couldn't give up the party live. Changes don't come easy when you haven't excepted God in your life.

God had now given me the job I aways wanted (I had the wife I needed), what more could I want? I don't think I even knew the asnwer to that one. I was still living in the dark (he who has eyes let them see), I was still unable to see.

By having a job this give us extra money coming in, now we could start looking for our own place. We were still living with my wife's oldest sister and her family. Their wasn't any problems living with them, we all got alone as one big happy family. Still every married couple needs their own place.

When we final did get our own apartment, it was close to where my father lived, when we lived with him before. Now we had our own place (Gold bless the child that's got his own). I still couldn't let go of the wild life (I was staying out all night), and partying all week-ends. Things seems to be get worst when they should be getting better.

I know "God" begin to see me as a hard case (even with his blessing's), I haven't changed. That's why he made a woman name, "Rutha M. Hall" she still had fate in me.

Our first apartment was at 6608 south Peoria, on the 3rd floor. It was an old apartment that needed work. Since it was our first apartment, we didn't mind helping fix it up. It was kind of fun during something together.

We had to paint the rooms, for the first month's rent. We only had furinture for, one bedroom, the living room, and the other rooms were empty.

Since this was our first apartment (we just love having our own place) for the first time since we had been married. We didn't mind the empty rooms at all, they seem full to us.

We had great 'times', at 6608 south peoria and then bad 'times', at 6608 south peoria. Through it all my wife stood strong. God was not present in my life (at the time) or I didn't 'recognize' him. Now I know he was there all the time.

My cousin, (who own the building) was living somewhere else with her husband and my father was living on the first floor at 6616 south peoria.

Something happen in her marriage. Maybe God wasn't present, (if he was) it wouldn't have broken.

Either way they broken-up, my cousin 'then', had to move back to 6616 south Peoria (on the first floor), and my father had to move back on the 2ⁿᵈ floor. This lasted for about 2 years, I guest God came back into their lives.

Then my coisin and her husband madeup, 'she then' moved back with him. My father then, moved back on the first floor, opening up the 2ⁿᵈ floor for us. I know this sound's like musical chairs but it really did happen that way.

We then, moved from 6608 south Peoria to 6616 south Peoria, for the 2ⁿᵈ time, on the 2ⁿᵈ floor, for the 2ⁿᵈ time. I know that sound's unreal but that to did happen. I still hadn't recognize 'God' in my life. I was still walking in the dark, running into everything, like a blind man with out a cain.

While living on the 2ⁿᵈ floor I begin to start seeing thing different. Like what a real man should be. Or shall I say what I though a real man should be.

This was the last time, I ever put my hand's on my wife 'I hit her in the eye', by excident, for that I'm sorry. And for all the other times before that (that was not an excident), I'm turly sorry. Please "for give me", for all those times, and the excident.

Because a real man don't hit a woman. With the help of 'God' I'm now becoming a real man.

Our life was very good living on peoria, (we had family gathering) cook-out's for the holidays, and parties for X-mas. All my wife's family excepted me as family (we were one big happy family) but something was missing (I had no son).

Then "God" made it possible for me to have one, "Tony", my son. Now everything was perfect (no such thing in life) as perfect, only "God" is perfect. So, he gave me the perfect son. Now life was good.

To show you how good God was (he gave us a daughter), her name was "Veronica better know as Putby" she always remember my birthday even if it was the day after Xmas, and never forgot me on father's day. That should made any man a happy man.

But even after 'God ' gave me a son, and daughter (I chose the street), over them. I missed out on their childhood running the streets. My wife did a very good job raising my son (with little help from me). For that I ask my son to give me. It's as 'if' my whole life has been asking someone to forgive me for

something 'or' saying I'm sorry. A good thing my daughter was raise by her real mother with help from my wife. Other wise I would be asking her forgiveness.

After my son graduated from high school, my wife and I decided to come together as a 'team', to made sure he graduated from ITT, and he did.

With all these blessing's I will surely change (not so), I still haven't seen the light (I was still during the same thing) partying all night. The streets had a hold on me and it wouldn't let go. It was like a junky on drugs. Something being a junky I knew alot about.

By now, God is saying, "I give up" but God never give's up on us (he sees things we don't). Like my wife seeing things in me (I couldn't see) or anyone else could see.

My stepmother became ill at this time and my wife took care of her (what a woman). This wounderful woman cared for, my stepmother, my father, and my mother until their death. There is that number again (3) trinty, meaning God in planning this.

After a long battle with cancer, my stepmother died. My father was still in a nursing home at the time. My wife and I, now had to visit my father in the nursing home twice a week to make sure he was being taken care.

Every week for 5 years (my wife took food) every saturday, so he could have something different to eat (other than nursing home food).

My mother was still living down south, her husband had died, and her stepchildren were now grown, so she moved to Chicago too live with us. My mother loved my wife as her own daughter and my wife love my mother the same. They were truly mother and daughter.

After my mother moved to Chicago, my wife was somewhat happy, again. They were like mother and daughter. This made me happy (also). Now God's plan was begin to work once more.

This was a match made in heaven. See, God is working his magic. Now I will surely change (no such luck), I was still a self center asshole, thinking I was God's gift to women.

IV. Our first home at 6616 south Peoria

❧⁂❧

MY WIFE AND I was living on the 2nd floor, my father, and my stepmother was living on the first floor. This would become our first home in Chicago. The first place I lived when I can to Chicago. Now God will made a way for me to own it.

My father had lived there for over 20 years before getting fired from his job as a contruction worker. He was very depress and started traveling alot. First he went to New York, and then down south where he had a stroke.

After the stroke, it left my father unable to talk or walk. He had to be put in a nursing home.

When my cousin decided to sell the building, she ask me, "if I wanted to buy it", I said, "yes", and the building was sold to my wife and I. Since it was a 2 flat building, I could rent out the 2nd floor.

After buying the building my wife's older sister move on the 2nd floor with her family. I was now a landlord (getting rent), from my own building. This was something I couldn't even dream of 2 years ago. But, I still couldn't see past 1 day, the future was like a blank space.

I still hadn't change from my old ways, partying all night, and chasing

women. I know God must be pulling his hair out saying, "what do I have to do too make this sin-er change?" keep my wife by my side, because she still had fate in me.

Then, my stepmother became ill with cancer and had to be cared for by my wife (what a good person), looking out for an 'asshole' like me and caring for my stepmother to. On top of that, she was helping care for my father in a nursing home.

After all the things I had done in the past (she was willing to care for my family in the future), I say it again, "what a woman". I thank God he put you in my life.

After a long battle with cancer my stepmother pass away. My wife and I, now had to care for my father in the nursing home. We would visit him 2 times a week to make sure the nursing home was taking care of him the right way. I would come every Wednesday and both of us would come every Saturday.

My wife took him food for 5 years (every Saturday) so he could have something other than the nursing home's food to eat. My father loved my wife's cooking (everybody did), she is a great cook. My neice once said, my wife could make a rock taste good.

I say it once again, "what a woman" with the strengh from God. He knew she would need it (with an asshole like me), because it would take a super woman to keep our ship on course.

My mother was still living down south, and then (her husband died). Since both her daughters were grown "Nicole & Hope", she moved back to Chicago (to live with us). This would give my wife some help with me, and my father.

My mother love my wife (like she was her daughter) and she loved my mother the same way (a match made in heaven). See, 'God' was still working his magic, because his 'power', is 'power'.

Now I will surely change (no such luck), still the same self center asshole I always was. What would it take to make me see the light too bring me from the darkness.

This must make God say, "I give up" but 'God' never give's up on 'us'. Only God, my mother, and my wife could have fate in a person like me. There's that number again (3) his plan is now enforce.

With all these blessing's from God, a wonderful wife, a son, and now my mother (what more could a person want)? Slowly change, 'did' begin to come.

I started taking my wife on vactions and we did other things together. We were begining to erase the past, the future was now looking bright. I was able to see the future beyond 1 day. I had come out of the darkness and started seeing some light.

Since my mother was now living with us (I made a proposition to her), what if we got my father out of the nursing home (to my surpise), they both said, "yes" before I finished the sentence.

My wife was now willing to allow my mother and father to live with us. No words can descript who this woman is, my wife (Rutha M. Hall) sent from "God". Because only a woman God sent could complete this task.

So, we had my father removed from the nursing home and was brought to our home.

my wife, mother, and I would now take care of him. The number (3) again, God was now forcing his plan into play.

With our help my father was able to get out of bed, dress himself, go to the bathroom, and feed himself on his own. He was now able to do all of this by himself.

He was in the nursing home for over 5 years and couldn't do any of this. I don't blame the nursing home, they couldn't make him do anything.

This was done after 1 year of being out of the nursing home, he was there for 5 years and was totally helpless when we brought him home. Now he could almost take care of himself.

My wife was a great care giver, for me, my mother, and my father. "WHAT" more can I say about this woman my wife, "thank you God".

After, about 5 years of being out of the nursing home, my father pass away. He died on his feet not lying on his back, 'helpless' in a nursing home. He died in the home where he always lived with both of us by his side.

God had allowed us, (to make him feel like a man) once again before he died, "thank you God", for that. Because only you have the 'power' to say when. He also cleaned the slate between father and son.

After that a change in me was starting to take hold. My love for the street was begining to vanish. I know longer think of myself as, "God's gift to women", just as a man (who has been truly bless). But my eyes were still close so I couldn't truly see.

My mother moved back down south after my father's death. She became home sick and wanted to go home (I understood), I once felt that way.

So, she returned back south and our live's returned back to nornal. I had now become somewhat responsible, our ship was on the right course, now that God was the 'navigator', my wife had always been the 'anchor', that held the ship in place.

Soon after my mother move back south she got married. This would be her 3rd marriage, the (1) for love. The 3rd time is the charm and the number (3) again. You can see God's hand at work.

I think this was the reason my mother wanted to return south (she found the man of her dreams). You're never to old to fall in love.

The marriage only last a short period of time (he died). This was her 3rd marriage but the most happiest, because it was about romance and love. She decided to stay down south after his death and buy a new home. She always wanted a new home where the family could come for holidays.

God was still blessing my mother (even after the death of her true love), my mother was a, 'saint'. I never had to worry about how she was doing, because she was a, 'saint' and God take's special care of them.

My wife is also a (good person) and God will do the same thing for her. That's why he put her in my life, once our ship is on course, I will take care of this good person, my wife "Rutha M. Hall".

After my mother built the new home of her dreams, in the location of her dreams (God allow her 5 years to enjoy her dreams), what a blessing. God allowed me to cook her last Thanks-giving dinner in her new home. This was the first time I never cook a full course meal and it turned out prefect. Only God came do prefect so now I know it was him all alone.

Then, my mother became "ill" and had to return to Chicago to live with me and my wife, (again). Nothing more in live (would make my mother happier) than to spend her last day's on earth with her son and daughter (God allow her to do that), 'see' I told you my mother was, 'a saint'. God had blessed her with all the blessing's she desired in life and now (even in death).

God sent 3 angels to care for her during her time of suffering, "Mae (my wife), Lou, and Tina" I will be forevery beholding to them. My heart reserve a special place for all (3), a dedit I can never repay. My wonderful wife was there from the beginning.

During this time, 'God' showed his sign, to me. He made my greatest fears my greatest joy. How may you ask? God allow me to be at the foot of my

mother's bed the night she died, this was my greatest fear (of not being there), my greatest joy (she gave me her final approval) of the person I had become.

I was no longer a self center asshole but the person my mother was proud to call, "her son". My wife was by her bedside the night she died also (I know she looked at my wife with a smile) as she said, "good by" when God lead her to heaven.

My mother's body was flown back down south for the funeral so she could be buried next to her husband #3, the love of her life.

During the funeral (I almost went into shock), at the idea of my mother's body being put in the ground. I broke down in tears at the very though. But that's what happen to someone after a funeral (they get put in the ground).

God knew what I was going through (he knows everything), he knew me even if I didn't truly know him. So, he cause it to rain until the grave was filled with water.

When the undertaker came in and said, "our mother's grave is filled with water, the burial will have to be later", my heart busted with joy. I couldn't stand to see my mother's body being put in the ground. God had spared me from that.

He had felt my pain and gave me relief (God recognize me even if I didn't recognize him) by sparing me that pain, thank you "God". But at the time I still didn't recognize him.

For the 3rd time God had tried to reach me, the 1st time, (when my father died), the 2nd time (when my mother died), and the 3rd time was after her funeral. But my eyes were still closed. What more would God have to do too make me see.

Although I didn't pray or go to church, "God" still recognize me (he knew what I was feeling all the time). He still loved me.

To show me, God did something even more wonderful after that (when we returned home) from the funeral.

After the funeral we all were sitting around, "talking" when this yellow rose (outside the door), caught everyone's eye (at the same time). It was the brightest 'shining' yellow rose, that anyone have ever seen. It was the spirit of our mother letting us know (I'm watching you). This made my eyes open wide now I can see the light.

After returning to Chicago (I could feel her spirit with me). Anytime I did

something wrong, I could hear saying, "Donny!!!" this help to keep my ship on course. God's plan was now working.

Then, because of all the things I had done in the past (my wife starting losing fate in me) and I don't blame her. It's hard to believe in someone that has hurt you, over, over, over, and over again. But now I had truly changed. I know saying it don't make it so, now I had to prove it.

Still my wife was in my corner (hoping the future would be bright).

This is were "God" tested her fate in me. He knew I had gained fate in him, 'so' God showed me the future. He allow me to see what would happen 5 years into the future. I know people may not believe that but he did.

God put our marriage to a test, by an act he lead me through (the foreclosure of our home at 6616 south Peoria), this was an act my wife couldn't understand, at the time.

God, had only showed it to me (she would have to have fate in me). God knew my wife believed in him but she now needed to believe in me (her husband). I had made her lose this fate so I had to be the one to restore it.

So, God took our home at 6616 south Peoria away (she became very, very angry at me), she didn't know this was God testing her fate in me that he had showed the future to me. Even when I told my wife, (the future would be alright) she still couldn't see. The only way she could see would be through me.

The message, God gave to me for my wife was, "have fate in God but believe in your husband", so, until she truly believe in me, I couldn't deliver God's message to her. I couldn't make her see so the angry grew.

We had lived at 6616 south Peoria for over 30 years (owing our own building), I know it was hard to walk away. My father first and then, my mother had both died there. I will always have great memories of living there, but all the value in the building was gone. God had show me, it was time to move on.

My mother and father had died in the same room (they could have reach out touch each other, they died that close), in the same room (at different times), after being apart for over 40 years. Is that not an act of God?

My mother and my father died under our roof (my wife and I), were both present at the time 'act of God'. Because only God can make those arrangement. He was showing me so I would know his power.

I tried to convince my wife of this, but she could only see her lost, (not the future) something she use to see in me (my future), now she couldn't see her's.

The day we moved (was a ugly day). My wife said things about me (that were very bad), she called me some name's (that was even worst). I didn't recognize this woman, what happen to the person I married?

What my wife didn't know (was), when you have 'earned' God's blessing's, you can't loss anything. Because the thing you though you have lost will be replaced with something even better. She couldn't see that at the time, only what was lost.

My wife felt like I had throwing away our future, she said, "that at our age I had got us put out in the street". We had a place to go, an apartment (1 building down) not block but building.

We didn't need a truck to move. We walk our belongs from 6616 south Peoria to 6608 south Peoria, on the same side of the street. Still able to get the mail from the same address. My wife still couldn't see God's plan working, anger blinded her.

We moving back into the same apartment we lived in before we moved to 6616 south Peoria, only this time the apartment at 6608 south Peoria was new. We were the first people to live there since it had been newly done. It was not like the fist time when we had to paint, this time it was very nicely done.

Before we moved that day, I made my wife a promise, I said "she would have a home, with a big back yard in 5 years", but all she could see was what she though she had lost. my promise didn't mean a thing at the time.

So, we moved to our new address, (1 building over) still able to pick our mail up at the same address Able to move without a truck, but still my wife was angry. She could only see that thing she though was lost.

She still refused to except God's message from me. The message about believing in her husband. The second she did that, her suffering would be over.

V. *Life at our old/new address 6608 south Peoria, for the 2nd time.*

❧

ONCE WE WERE BACK at the old/new apartment, things got even worst. My wife couldn't stand to even hear the name "6616 south Peoria" with out breaking down in tears.

We were now back at the place we came from before it was 'old' now it's 'new'. I could feel "God" was trying to show us something. Everything felt so right for the first time in my life.

I tried to explain this to my wife (she was blind with angry), she refuse to listen. All my wife could see was what she though she had lost not what the future my hold.

I told her, "this was God redirecting our lives", but she didn't think I knew God well enough to say that (since I didn't pray or go to church).

She was right (in a way), I didn't know him well enough but God knew me well enough, because he knows everything. I'm learning him more and more each day (the things God have done and showed me), I can no longer deny his existing.

When we lost our home, it was as 'if' she lost a member of the family.

If only she could have seen, what I saw (the future in 5 years) but she didn't believe in me so how could she receive "God's" message from me.

I knew what the message was, 'but' God hadn't showed me how to make it happen. I though I knew, 'but' I was wrong. I had to wait the full 5 years before finding out (God was testing my fate in him), he had shown me his power's were almighty, and still I didn't believe.

When my father died, "God" erased all the bad feelings (I had about him) and replace them with 'love'. Only God have the power to do that.

When my mother died, (God allowed me to be at the foot of my mother's bed) and be the last person she saw (except my wife), before closing her eye's 'forever'.

Someone once ask me, "who do I thing God is"? At the time I didn't know the answer but now I do. The answer is, "everything". God is everything that exist on earth and in heaven. Nothing is unknown to God, because he sees and knows everything.

The place we had moved to was the same place we lived, on the same floor, and the same apartment 30 years ago before moving too 6616 south Peoria. I told my wife this was the waiting stage until God found the prefect place for us. What I said didn't mean one thing. The future was blind to her.

The number (3) is a holy number because of trinity (father, son, holy spirit), I could clearly see "God's" plan at work. Because the number (3) keeps coming up.

My wife was still blind, (to what she though) she had lost. I tried to explain too her, "that you have to let go of the past, in order see what the future has in store". To no avail, just the sound of the name, "6616 south Peoria" was enough to make her break down and cry. Only time could erase such pain.

After a year had pass, my wife could finally hear the name, "6616 south Peoria" without causing tears. She could now walk pass (take a look), without feeling she had lost something. My wife even begin to love our new apartment.

Then, a family moved in at 6616 south Peoria, this made her final give up the idea of moving back, "thank you God". I know it was you, because I couldn't.

The owner had tried to sell the building but had no buyer's, so he had to rent it out.

This removed the dream of going back from her mind, so now we could move on, I hope.

The address at 6616 south Peoria is now behind us, it took over a year for my wife to get over it but she final did. God final open her eye's to that (leave the past behind) so you can see the future.

After the grieving was over, our life at the new apartment was very good. We starting back having family gathering on holiday's again. There were no backyard cook out's but 3rd floor BBQ. Things had got back to normal (at our new apartment).

I had claims in with the VA (that once are granted), our problems would be solved.

This was now I though "God's" message of how to was (to buy the new home with the big back yard). But I was wrong again.

I had got my wife hope's up (many times in the past before), about what I was going to be getting (from the VA) to end up disappointed.

This time I though it was real, (I though this was "God's" plan), so how could it not be granted? But it wasn't "God's" plan, it was mine.

The day I received the letter from the VA (before I open it), I knew it would be denied, and it was. A voice in my head had told me that it would be denied and what to do next.

My wife had called and ask me, "did the letter from the VA come", I said, "yes", she ask, "what was the decision"? I didn't know how to answer.

So, I final said, "it was denied", I could sense her disappointment. I told her not to worry, I had another plan (this time it is God's plan).

After being denied by the VA, my wife couldn't see any other way for us to get what I had promise in 5 years (a new home with a big backyard). I knew it would happen.

God had showed me how to make it happen (my wife couldn't see this), she still didn't believe in me so I still couldn't deliver "God's" message to her. Once she believed, all her problems would be over.

This is when, "God" put a little angel in our lives (a little girl "Akria"). I remember when I first saw her, I said, "I'm not going to babysit someone else baby", but the baby had a different idea.

When my wife first ask me to hold her, I held her like a loaf of bread.

She looked at me with the most beautiful eyes, 'like magic'. Before I knew what happen, I was holding her close in my arms. She put her little arm around my neck and pulled me even closer (I was hooked), like a fish on a line.

My wife, after finishing what she was doing, said, "I can take her now", I said, "I got this", and the rest is history.

About 3 months after (the bad decision) from the VA of the denial, "God" showed me how to keep my promise too my wife and buy that new home with a big back yard.

This was 5 years (from the day I promise her), when we left 6616 south Peoria, what I would do (get her a home with a big back yard), now I have done it.

God showed me how (to keep the promise), I made too my wife in the time he said he would (5 years).

When we first went to look at our new home, it did have a big back yard. I knew from first sight, this was the home "God" had prepare for us.

Once I was sitting in our back yard, 'looking up at the trees', I saw what I had seem, when I was a young boy (growing up in the south), the same view (I saw then), 'I see now' in the trees in our back yard. That's why I know "God" directed us here.

What I saw then and see now (trees that blocked out the sky), I saw the same view as a young boy, in our back yard (62 years later). If this is not "God's" plan, then there is no such plan.

I felt, I was being pushed by something 'the wind', my wife, and I was being 'navigated' by someone "God", that's why my ship reach it's destination (a new home with a big back yard). God's promise kept.

VI. *Moving to our new home at 9304 south Vanderpoel.*

❦

WHEN WE MOVED IN *our new home on December 2, 2012 (it was on a Monday morning), the reason the date stick is (the day we moved in), the gas company cut off our gas. It was very cold that day (my bill was paid), but the gas company had to transfer my gas over from the old address to the new address. They said it wouldn't be turn off with the transfer, but it was.*

It took 2 weeks for the gas company to turn it be on, we had to buy electric heaters to keep warm. We had our new home but had to suffer for the first 2 weeks in a cold house. I can't understand why it took so long when the bill was paid.

After that thing's got normal and we were able to truly settle into our new home. We begin to furnish all the rooms and our new home became (home). But my wife's family (and mine) seemed to be distance. It's as if we moved out of their lives (that we had did something wrong), cause we got a new home. I though they would be happy for us but seem they weren't.

I told my wife, "that when someone need a place to stay, things would change" and it did.

During that time "God" allow his little angel "Akria" to live with us. This made our new home more of a home, "God" knew that, because he knows everything. A house without kids is not a home, it's just a house.

As I said before, someone asked me, "who do I think God is"? God is "everything" the past, present, and the future. Just like the number (3), "trinity" the sign of "God", I began to see the number (3) everywhere. It became my lucky number.

Since this is a question no man has a right to ask another man (only God can ask that question), because only "God" knows the right answer.

Because only someone that knows everything, knows the answer to that question. The only one I can think of, "is God", what he see's in (one man), he might not see in (another). That's why man can not judge man. Man can't see the life of man, what he may become in the future, only God can see that. That's how he shows us how to fix things.

So, to try and bring the family back together, my wife and I gave a cookout for the holidays. This was to try to get things back the way they were when we were all one big happy family.

The whole family came and we were back being a family again. We never stop being a family, but what ever difference were resolved. We were now a real happy family, same as before.

My son, "Tony" was in and out, so "God" put other little angel in our lives "Lee–Lee".

Another little girl with magical eyes (that stole our heart), now their was 2 little angels sent from "God", as a blessing for us. This made our new home even more of a home, filled with the love of a new little angel.

God knows the things we truly want in our heart (because he knows everything), and if we are living by his plan (those thing that we want in our heart), he will make happen.

My wife and I, have always want a little girl. To show you how "God" works, we kept the grandmother of the 2 little "angels" when she was little "angel". We wanted to raise her.

The father of this little angel wouldn't allow us to raise her, this hurt my wife very badly. She cried for weeks, "God" knew her pain. Because, "God" knows everything, he knew I wasn't ready to help raise a child (I was still a child myself).

So, "God" delayed his blessing until we both were ready (now me more

than my wife), she had already raise kids (with my son and her sisters kids). This was new territory for me but I was ready for the journey.

Then "God' decided to test of resolve, he tested our will to summit. He created division (I know most people don't think God do that) but he do. He tests us to see if we were ready for the task he had planed for us. Since God knows our minds and when we are ready (we will know) because he already knows.

God cause (my wife's mind) and (my mind), 'to go' in the directions it wanted. He allowed our mind's to go in it's own direction. Both our minds went in different directions. We begin to become farther apart. We couldn't agree on anything, 'If' I said "right, she would say, "left". Things became worst instead of better.

So then, "God" decided to do something different. I was leaving my wife alone everyday, we were becoming more and more 'distant'. We had be married for over 30 years but now we were like someone that never met and different.

My wife was becoming lonely and feeling isolated. God could see this (because he see's everything), so he did something.

God created a situation were my wife's baby "sister and her husband " had to come live with us. This made my wife very happy (it made me happy also), because now my wife wouldn't feel so isolated, and alone.

But after awhile I begin to feel like an outsider, they had so much fun talking about, "where they grew up", I grew up something place else. I couldn't be apart of the conversation, 'so' I felt left out. This made me feel like an outsider in my own home.

My wife love having bible discussing with them (but not with me), it was as 'if' I didn't know God so how could I be talking about the bible. How can another person say who knows "God", and who don't? This is the problem with people of fate, (they think) they speak for God (only God specks for God).

This seem to cause even a greater distance between my wife and me. She said it was because, "I had a problem with her family living here", but it wasn't. I loved having them live here, because it made her happy. The problem was with us, (not with them) living with us.

Then God decided, that this testing wasn't working, he then provided a place for my wife's family to live. So they moved someplace else. God knew it wouldn't work since he knows everything, it was to show us (it was us).

After her sister and husband had moved away, things begin to get even worst. Then their was no one else to blame (but us). This cause things to reach a boiling point. Our home had become a bomb waiting to go off.

Then my son and I had a difference of agreement, and I was 'so' angry I attacked him. Since "God" knows everything, he saw this coming to. He arranged for it to happen in a place where we couldn't hurt each other In the bathroom (in the bath tub).

There is very little room in a bath tub to fight. This allow both of us to get rid of pin-up angry. Minutes after it was over (I realize how wrong I was), I met my son on the way to saying I'm sorry (coming to say he was sorry), we hugged and we both said, "I'm sorry". I then promised him it would never happen again.

God had just made things right between me and my son, "Tony". My wife was horror stricken 'so' was our (2) little angels 'by' what had just happen, at first she could only see what had just happen, later she saw what had really happen (God brought my son and I), together 'forever'.

Still my wife was carrying weight she didn't have to carry. She still didn't truly believe in me, so the message "God" gave me to give her (I couldn't give). She was still suffering needlessly because of this.

The minute she started to truly believe (all of her worries would be over). This was "God's" promise to me, but she had to be the "one", too come to that point (until then she will remain suffering).

Then came angel #3 with angel eyes, "Fat Fat", the number (3) again, "trinity" for the 3ʳᵈ time (father, son, holy spirit). A blind man can now see, that this is "God's" plan.

So, I did like Moses (when he went on the mountain top and "God" spoke to him) by the burning bush.

I to, have a burning bush (on my mountain), so, I went on my mountain and "God" reveal something to me. God reveal these thing to me.

1. *He show me how to get my total compensation from the VA.*
2. *Then write a book telling my story, he show me how it should be written.*
3. *Then he show me how to start my own company.*
4. *Then he show me how to write it up from the top down and then get it started from the bottom up, he had shown me the top.*

5. Then "God" show me how to start fixing the problems between my wife and me.

6. He reveal to me "that both of us was right", how can that be was my first though, he then reveal something else to me, that was even more confusing "because we or who we are", this puzzle me even more.

On my next trip to my mountain top, "God" made it plan to me. He spelled it out in plan words, "both of you are right being who you are", now agree to disagree, stop saying who's right or wrong (both of you are right), that's the reason you were chosen. Now work it out, was "God's" command.

We did work it out, now my wife and I finish each others sentences (about the right things), we agree to disagree about things we may think different of. Now our directions are no longer going in different directions but in a circle that will meet in time.

I have now made that 62 year journey, from when I was a 5 year old boy, to a 67 year old man (too the place), "God" had shown me, as that 5 year old boy.

When you make it to the place that "God" has shown you (your blessing are there), and will be there 'forever'. This is called heaven on earth.

Then, I went on my mountain top again, and "God" reveal to me that there were greater goals ahead. The 3 little angel's future (that's why he showed me how to build something for them), and give me a true purpose in life.

This book was written to take us through the story of our live (in hopes of forgiveness), and show you, how sorry I am for all the wrong things, I did in the past. I can't change the past, I can only learn from it (going forward). Because of the past our marriage will be like a rock in future.

For the rest of my life, I will do everything in my power to made up for the past, 'so' please forgive me for that and except me for the future.

We became aware, (my wife and I) that "God" was testing our 'will's', he saw our will's couldn't be broken (our marriage maybe). So, "God" made our 'will's' as one 'will', and our marriage became (rock solid).

I know "God" still have higher goals for us. With your 'wind' and God's 'navigation', we will reach those goals together.

Since God, knows everything, see's everything (from now until forever), he knew this would happen (he had to make us know).

Because now I recognize, that "God" was their in the beginning (he allowed me to be me), and when I was ready, "God open my eye's", so I could see.

I tried all I could (to deviate) from 'God's plan', but when it's 'God's plan' (it is the plan).

A lot of people today that call themselves saved (are worst off now than when they became saved). Who saved you? God point you in the right directions (not the wrong directions). So, it may not be God that saved you.

When you are saved by "God" you can't go in the wrong directions 'no' matter how hard you try. I'm living proof of that.

I now know why people who think they know "God" feel saved, 'but' or you save on earth? When you have been saved by God 'no' earthly thing can harm you (the greatest blessing of all).

When you have been faced with death (when you should have been killed) something save you, then you have been saved. Because that something that saved you was "God ".

My mother use to call me a mercy baby, (the reason why my father's father shot him in the head at point blank range) he suppose to be dead (this was before I was conceded). People said it was because the gun was to close to his head. I now know the reason (God blocked the shot), he saved me before I was born. Just like he saved Danial in the lions den, he saved me. When you are saved by "God" no earthly thing can harm you. Man can't say, "no" to death (only God), his angels will protect you from death (when you are saved) by God on earth.

God sacrificed his only son "Jesus" for the sins of man 'so' man could be free to live his own life. He give man the opportunity to believe in him 'or' not. So, if you believe in God (live a righteous life), you will be saved in heaven.

So, by praying (going to church) want save you. This is something else man do to serve (man). God will save you with your last breath (accept him as your savior) 'no' matter how you have lived.

Man have always served (man), God's says "you can't serve 2 masters" that's why he sent angels to serve him.

Man can't save himself from earthly 'or' heavenly things 'so' how can me

save you? Man can not save man (only God can do that) the second you except him has your savor.

What if the man that was trying to save you wasn't saved himself. Man look at the sky for the second coming (what if he's already here), what if you walk by him today 'or' the day before. God will come when man lest expects him (you make not recognize him) 'so' be ready for him always.

By praying, going to church, and being so called saved (don't make you know "God". I do none of these 3 things (the number 3 again), "trinity", meaning "God" has spoken.

But going to church, praying, and fate/save is also the number 3, "trinity" God has spoken. So, how can I know "God" and not do these 3 things? I have a direct line to him, this avoid any confusion. I know exactly what his 'message' is for me.

I now know who God is (most men that thank they do), should know (you can't keep anything from him), because God 'see's' and 'knows' everything (he is everything).

So, my wife "Rutha M. Hall" and I, are now 'God's plan' from the beginning, to the ending.

The poker game of life 'is' the hardest one tho win (unless God is the dealer). Because when you play the hand (that God deals), you can't lose.

My wife and I was talking about the reason so many kids are being killed today, I ask, "why would God allow this to happen?" She said, "it's not God it's man", I said, "but God knows everything so he knew it was going to happen, why didn't he stop it?". Then it occurred to me (thousands of kids are killed everyday) they are our future. So, God is trying to show man that without kids there is no future. Because he works in ways man will never understand, until man summit to God.

When I was growing up, I had a saying, "live fast die young have a good looking corpus". I did everything in my power throughout the years to make that a true statement. I now know why I failed. God had his arms around me then.

Three times God showed me death, the first time when I was young, the second time in Vietnam, but the third time he made me know it was him who saved me. I was trapped in the door of my car with it in gear and moving (I couldn't stop it), someone came from (I don't know from where) he stop the

car, and was gone. I can't explain it, but this is what happen. God sent an angel to save me.

Then, he showed me in a vision (that he saved me the 2 other times). The first time, when I was young some people tried to kill me (3) times with a razor and gun (shooting at me 6 times missing all 6), God saved me by making the (6) shot miss, and not allowing them to have seven. The second time in Vietnam a VC terrorist tried to kill me (3) times the third time God controlled my shots (I shot at him 6 times all hitting him) killing him. God made their shots miss and my shots hit.

Twice the Devil tried to take me (the number 6, the number of shots 6,6), God said, "no" but the third time he tried to take me "God" sent his angel to save, and protect me. This meant (6) evil, against (3) Trinity (God wins), and sent (3 little angels).

Throughout my life, I have been comp-ailed to do the right thing, although I did a lot of wrong things (how can the be) the Devil was trying to take my soul, but God won.

So, my message from "God" to man ' is' "get your life in order, then everything else will be in order, then you will be playing a winning hand".

Remember God is ' everything' he knows everything, so you can't lie to him only to yourself. He knows your inter-most thoughts 'so' be very careful of what you think.

Now I'm going to say something that will 'piss off" all people that think they're saved. Man can not serve God (get over the shock), because God's needs are beyond man's understanding therefore he sent angels to earth to serve him (I know, an angel saved me). However you can come to truly know God and be saved (after death). Death is eternal mind 'so' if your mind is a Godly mind (you live in heaven forever).

So, man can only serve man (by living a righteous life), because man only knows the needs of man (God knows the needs of everything). So, going to church "or' praying don't mean you have lived a righteous life (but God knows). The second you except God has you savor (you are saved), he will make your mind (a righteous mind).

Man is already serving 3 masters, his addictions to money, sex, and violent s. God said, "you only serve 1" so how can man serve God when he's already serving 3?

Because God knows everything (he knew man could never truly serve

him), the faults of man or to great (greed, selflessness, pride) would keep man from serving God. To be saved is to except God as your savor (period).

God don't save man through man, he save man by the power of God. When he saved you on earth, then you become one of his angels on earth (same as Jesus) to serve him (same as the angel of death). That don't mean you shouldn't be good (you will be judge later). When you have been saved on earth (you are saved in heaven) no need to be judged.

However God do save you through someone else 'if'' that someone else has been saved by God. People like (mother's, father's, preachers) that serve 'people' that God save (will be saved) in heaven.

When you are truly saved all earthly things that try to harm you will be removed (by angels) sent 'by' God from heaven to protect you. Each time someone tried to harm me (they were harmed the same way) they tried to harm me (angels).

My mother told me, "the night I was born, she almost died, then she saw God". I don't know if this is true or not (but that's what she told me). When you almost die (then see God) you have been saved at that second. My mother was saved the night I was born.

People read the bible 'but' don't truly understand it's meaning, the Lords prayer "on earth as it is in heaven", when you have been saved (by God) on earth, then you have been saved in heaven.

For a long time I could not understand why God would allow my brother to be killed and not me (since I was in Vietnam where being killed in normal), but now (I think), I understand (God had plans for us) Rutha M. Hall and me.

So, I summit to him (then realize he was in control all along), and allowed "God", to lead 'us' my wife and I too the place he prepare for us (9304 south Vanderpoel), heaven on earth where blessings are forever. Now I'm no longer lost (God allow me to find him) 'so' I could find myself.

When God have taken you through your life (shown you he was there all along) how can you not–believe? God made me believe 'now' I know God saved me 'or' I wouldn't be here today. He loved me then (more than I loved myself).

Because when you are successful through God (you are truly successful), "on earth as is in heaven" so says God,

To see God's promise kept go to YouTube @ "Donnell home".

"3" little angels, a blessing from "God"

What they mean in our life

Before I start with this part, I want to tell you a story of how much these "3" little angels mean to me. When God give's you a blessing, he sometimes test you to see, 'if' you desire it or not. Blessings are something we have nothing to do with, like these "3" little angels. Something I had nothing to do with.

God tested his most fatefull follower, 'by' giving him a son, then asking him "to give him up", this was testing his fate. What if, it was not his son. Would the man do the same thing?

This is the test God put to me, he made it seem as though, "the 3 little angels" he blessed us with, would be take away. We had them for the summer, thinking it was the last summer, we might every see them again. This was like someone cutting my heart out, (with a knife) it would kill me just as dead 'if' they were taken away.

The place they were suppose to be taken too, they didn't want to go, and they didn't like the people they were going with. So, noway was I

going to allow that too happen, over my dead body. God knows your heart, he knows your actions, and he knows what you will do,

Then, I went on my mountain and told God, what I was willing to do, I said "I would kill the people that are trying to take them away, I would call the police and say I did it" then they would be give to their father (the family). Then I know they will be taken care off.

God's knows your heart (he knows everything), 'so' he knew, "I was willing to do this". Then, I made a promise with God, 'if' he made this go away, I would be there for them, the rest of my life. So, God did make this go away, now I will keep my promise to him, always.

God, tested me right off the bat, he made me there driver (to and from school) the rest of that year, and the next. They would boss me on the way there and on the way back, "stop at McDonald's", or "take me to the park". I had now become their personal driver.

Then little angel "3" became apart of the act. She started her first day of School, Tuesday 5, 2017, alone with the other "2" little angels for their 2nd school year. Now all "3" of my little angels are headed in the right directions.

This was a future I couldn't see, even if I had been looking in a crystal ball. But this is a future I would kill or be killed 'to keep'. So, if there are no more blessings in my life, God have given me the greatest blessing, he can restore on any man. I will alway's (for as long as I live) be thankful to God, for my "3" little angels 'sent by him'.

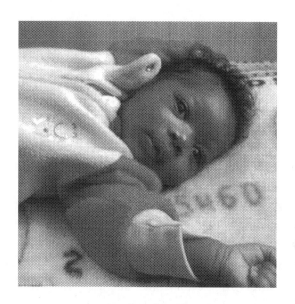

VII. *Little angel # 1, "Akria Brooks"*.

WE WERE LIVING AT 6608 south Peoria, on the the 3rd floor, when this little angel came into our life's. I remember when I first saw her, she was only 2 months old, her name was "Akria Brooks". The first thing that came to my mind was, "I not going to baby sit no baby" I didn't even want to hold her.

My wife was doing something in the kitchen and ask me, "to hold her" I really didn't want to hold her, "so" I held her like a loaf of bread. She looked at me with the eyes of an angel, it changed something in side of me. My heart felt a sense of warmth, that cause my body, to feel warm all over.

She then put her little arms around my neck, pulling me close to her, and then smile with such a warm smile. The spell was casted, I was hooked like a fish on a line. When my wife finished what she was during and came back to get her, I said "I got this", I didn't want to put her down.

In only a couple of minutes, "it was like" we had known each other, for the 2 whole months, she's been in the world. This little angel was

playing with my mouth, sticking her finger in my ear, and rubbing my head "like she had known me, all her short life".

It was like love at first sight, between a 65 year old man, and a 2 month old little angel. I became her "Prince Charming", she chose me to be that, when she was just 2 months old. This little angel was living next door at 6610 south Peoria, on the 3rd floor "next door".

The baby I said, "I wouldn't baby-sit", I couldn't wait "to see", everyday now. Her father would drop her off in the morning's. He had brought her a stroller. When she came in, I could hear the stroller hitting the front door, and I knew it was her. When she saw me her whole face would light up, and so would mind. We both brought joy, to each other's life.

Before this little angel looked into my eyes, with that magic spell, I didn't really like being around kids much. I was a only child, I wasn't use to being around kids. This little angel changed all that, with just one look, "into my eye's".

With that look, she change my heart. A little angel sent from "God" to warm my heart. I could feel something special in her, I told my wife, "she is going to be someone special". My wife said, "I hope she don't break your heart". I said, "she want". Because she was a little angel sent by "God" to do something special.

Not long after that, "God" gave us another blessing. He gave us a home, so we would have a place to help raise his little angel. This was the home that we both dream of, a big back yard, and designer kitchen. Something we both wanted very bad, "God" knew this when he blessed us with this. Because he blessed us with this to taken care of his little angel. As long as we do this, we will always, "be blessed".

Our new home was located at 9304 south Vanderpoel, God had blessed us with the home of our dreams. We moved in December 3, 2013. I remember the date, "because" when we move in, our gas was cut off. Instead of transferring it over from the old address to the new address, the gas company, just cut it off.

God knew this, so his little angel wasn't with us during this time. We had to buy heaters and electric blanks to keep warm, this was the longest 2 weeks, I never seen. If you every stayed in a cold house, in the winter time, "in Chicago" you know what I mean.

After the 2 weeks, the gas company came out and cut our gas back on, then we could begin, "to" enjoy our new home. This was for the whole month of December, so ther weren't much of a X-mas that year.

The start of the new year January 2014, we were able to get our new home fully furnished. Now the little angel sent to us by God, could come stay in her new home. Everything had now been made ready.

So, in Febuary 2014 this little angel could come to her new home. Our bedrooms were on the 2nd floor, there were stars leading from the 1st floor up to the 2nd floor, we had to get a gate, "to put accross" at top of the stars. This little angel would crawl from "1" bedroon to the other, "so" the gate kept her, from crawling down the stars.

There were "3" bedrooms on the 2nd floor, this gave the little angel, alot of rooms to crawl around in, and she was crawling from one room to the other. She was only "1" year's old, but very aware, and very active.

This little angel had chose me as her, "Prince Charming" it's like I made her world light up. She would stay with me in a cold shack, "as long as" she could see me, she was happy. My wife and I were sleeping in our own rooms, she wanted us to sleep in the same room with her, "so" we had to do this, until she went to sleep.

She would push my wife over, almost out of the bed, to make room for me. Then, get in between us and hug me, while rushing my wife away. She was just "1" year's old, but it was like she wanted me "all to herself", even at that age.

We kept this little angel for most of the month of Feduary 2014, "but" as much as she loved us, she loved her, monnie "Vicky", and her dad-dad "Alanzo" more, "after all" they were her parents.

She want to go home with them, they want her to come home, "so" this little angel went home in March, 2014. When she left, I felt a lost feeling, a feeling of sadness, and loneness. Even though, we knew she would be coming back, it still left a empty void, when this little angel, "left".

We were still getting thing together at our new home, "so" this did help somewhat. By trying to get things together, we didn't miss her as much in the day time, but we really missed this little angel at night. She was going for about a month, "but" it seemed like a year.

In early April, 2014 the little angel came back to live with us,

nothing in life could have made me more happier. I think little angel "2" was on the way. This cause little angel "1" to have too spend the summer with us, this made my summer. She would follow me everywhere, all summer long. A summer, I will remember, for the rest of my life.

I took alot of pictures on my phone, to remmeber the summer by, "then" my phone my fell in the water, and all of my pictures were destoryed. But I still have them in my head, when I close my eyes, I can still see her, "as" that "1" year old little angel, running, and playing in my back yard. This will always be store in my mind, "so" I can relive, when I'm older, and grayer.

The summer went by very quickly, before we knew it, "it" was X-mas, December 2014. This was our first real family gathering, in our new home, at 9304 south Vanderpoel.

All of the family was there, her father, "dad-dad" was sitting on one side of the room, I was sitting on the other side, this little angel would run from him to me, "then" I moved when she wasn't looking, "when" she ran from him to me, she didn't see me, she was standing in the middle of the floor, looking all around, some one said, "what's she looking for?", her dad-dad said, "she's looking for Donny", that's what this little angel call me, "Donny".

After the X-mas party was over, her dad-dad was ready to leave, and want to take her with him. She starting crying, then ran to me, I think it was because, all the X-mas presents hadn't be open, "so" he decided to let her stay. She stayed with us until after the holiday's.

Her dad-dad came to get her January, 2015. Our little angel was gone for another month, that seemed like a year. We didn't have anything to do, too keep our minds off her. During this time, little angel "2" was born. We hadn't seem her, yet. It would be almost a year later before little angel "2", would come into our lives.

So, little angel "1" came back to stay with us awhile, until little angel "2" was more developed. When she came back, my wife said, "some new sleeping arraingement had to be made", my wife snored, I snored, and the littlie angel "1" snored even louder. No one could get any sleep.

Then I went back to my room, this little angel starting crying saying, "I want to sleep with Donny!!, I want to sleep with Donny!!!"

until my wife said, "go" she jump out of her bed, ran to mind, and jumped in. She crawl up next to me, "smiling" like she just won a prize.

I didn't know then, this little angel was staking her claim. She knew little angel "2" was coming soon. At the tender age of "2", this little angel came up with a plan, and started carrying it out. I didn't know that then, but I know it now.

So, when I wonder who chose, "who" I stop wondering, because I now know, "she chose me" I didn't choose her, because when she chose me, "I had no chose".

This picture, show's little angel "1" letting little angel "2" know who's on first. She's letting her know, "I looked into his eyes first, he belone to me, I'm not sharing", but, I love both of you equally. Maybe someday for different reason, "but" my love for both of you will always be the same.

I made a promise to, "God" if he did what I ask, and he did. So, now I will keep my promise to him (to be there for them) too death, and the

hereafter. When I reach death, I will have kept my promise, and God will decided the hereafter.

Then God showed me that little angel "1" was God sent. She was born Decmber 17, I was born December 26, nine days apart "3+3+3=9", God has spoken.

I was talking with little angel "1", I said "you are seven now when you get 12 you be a teenager' she said, "teenager's die" I said, "why would you say something like that?' she said, "because they get themselves in trouble". When a seven year old is afraid to reach 12 something in the world is very wrong.

VIII. *Little angel 2, "Aaliyah Brooks" better know as "Le-Le".*

❦

LITTLE ANGEL *"1"* HAD plans before little angel "2" even arrived. They both were with their parents during this time. But little angel "1" had spent most of the year of 2014 with us, she had stake her claim, and was willing to fight to keep it. She let little angel "2" know before she met me, I belone to her, and she wasn't willing to share.

It was on a Friday afternoon in late 2014, when I first met little angel "2", I didn't know what to expect. This little angel had being stating with her, "Ganner" this what they called their grandmother, "Annette".

She was one year old (little angel "2") the other little angel "1" was two years old, both were walking, and talking very well. I could see right away little angel "2" was born to run, my little track star. When she came in the door, she ran directly to me, and sit in my lap.

Little angel "1" sit on the other lap, trying to push little angel "2" off my lap, I made her just sit there. I knew then, little angel "1" didn't

want to share me with, little angel "2". So, the contest was on, to see who would win.

We had mixed up their own room, with their special chairs, and flate screem TV. A room fit for two little angels, a nice big bed, they both could sleep confortable in. But little angel "1" had her plans in mind already, she made her move first.

When night came (she act like), she was afraid of the dark. So, we had to have a night light installed. During the night, little angel "1" would wake-up calling my name, "Donnie !, Donnie !!, Donnie !!!" the 3rd time I had to come.

She want me to come get her and put her in my bed. She did this to make sure little angel "2" didn't make that move, first. As I said, "she had a plan at 2 years old and was carrying it out". What a smart little girl, bacause at the time, I didn't know what this little angel was doing. I knew, she would live with me (in a empty shack), with nothing in it (but me), and that would be enough for her.

But when little angel "2" ran to me that first day, she touched my heart also. Both had the eyes of an angel, with one look I was hooked, just like before. Now I had two little angels that I would give up my freed, or die for. But still little angel "1" didn't want to share her "Prince Charming", with anyone. My wife said, "she didn't even want to share me with her".

So, little angel "1" was able to convince my wife, she was afraid of sleeping with the light on, now one had to sleep with her, and the other one with me. Guest who little angel "1" want to sleep with? If you said, "me". You were right, this was her plan all along. This way she would have me all to herself. It worked, for then. This 2 year old little angel, had out smarted two grown-up's.

I rememeber one morning when I got up before she woke-up, I was in the room with little angel "2", she was sitting on my lap. I was putting on her shoes. When little angel "1" woke-up, came into the room, the look on her face, 'when' she saw little angel "2" sitting on my lap (like I had cheat on her).

Then little angel "1" starting crying, and ran back into her room. I had to explain to her, 'that' I loved them, 'both'. She made sure after that

(that little angel "2") never woke-up before her, again. Even at two years old (going on three), this little angel "1" had the ability to plan ahead.

I call little angel "2" my track star, I knew she had the ability when she was one year's old. She was playing in the bed with a dresser near the bed (the dresser moved), she was left hanging with her hands on the dresser, and her feet in the bed. I heard her calling for help, when I got to the room, she had held on, as long as she hold. I made it there in the neck of time. I knew then if little angel "2" could hold on that long (without falling), she had strong hands, and feet. This was the making of a track star, great hands, and feet.

I think little angel "2" had figured out that sitting next to me made little angel "1" angry, 'so' she did it just to make her angry. Both of these little angels were smart for their ages. But this did made an (66 year old man) heart feel warm inside. To have two little angels, love me that much, "I knew", I had to be doing something right, for "God" to bless me like this.

If I had looked into a crystal ball, I never could have seem this. This was something we had nothing to do with, somehting we couldn't vision, something we wouldn't normanly have a right to. But, in this case, it was "God" who determind these rights.

Most of the year of 2014, both the little angels spent a great deal of the time with us. I think little angel "3' was in the making. The other two little angels compete with each other for everything.

It wasn't we that was so special (it's a civil rivarly), something I knew alot about. My brother and I went through the same thing when we were going up. So, this part wasn't new to me. My brother and I were 10 months apart, we compete until we were teenagers.

I watch them compete over me, over toys, over food, over watching TV, and over everything else. My brother and I had done the same thing, until we were teenagers. So, I knew they to whould grow out of it. Watching them compete made the year 2014 go by very fast.

My wife and I had brought them a big doll house for X-mas. We spent a whole day putting it together, they didn't spend that X-mas with us. So, it was after X-mas before they had a chance to see it.

When they saw it (it was already put together) the only thing they could do with it was, 'play with it' or 'rip it apart', they decided on

ripping it apart. What had taken us all day and part of the night (putting together), these little angels, 'ripped apart' in 10 minutes.

Then I told my wife, "next time, we would let them put it together". Smart kids like these two little angels want to know how things are made, and what make them work. Smart kids are like that, I was like that. These "2" little angels loved hanging out with me.

So, I decided to take them with me to the race track, they loved it. They were racing with the horse's, buying refreshments form vending machines, and even reading the racing forms. These little angels were only one and two years old at the time. They both had great awareness and understanding about almost everything.

Everytime after that, when I would leave, they would ask, "are you going to the track, I want to go", now they were hooked on the race track at one and two years old. The good thing, they're not old enough to be bettting money, like me. But they did bring me luck, the first time I took them. But still playing the horse's is not a good idea, 'so' this is something I wouldn't want them to do.

One day little angel (2) ask me, "why did you jump on Tony?" I said, "I was wrong it will never happen again", she said, "but why did you do it?' I though she had forgot. Children never forget bad things that happen around them or to them. So, be very careful of what you do and say around your kids.

Little angel "1" have the smarts to change the game (she can become whatever), the world is her's to choose from. Little angel "2" will control the track, she was born to run, and will run until her goals are reached.

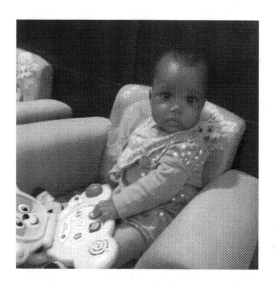

IX. *Little angel "3", "Amelia Brooks" better know as "Fat-Fat".*

❦

THIS LITTLE ANGEL WAS a year old, before she came to stay with us. She had spent a whole year during nothing but eating, and during #2. This little angel couldn't even walk, after being a year old. The two other little angels could talk, and run when they were a year old. This little angel didn't do nothing but crawl on floor like a fat pig. She couldn't talk, walk, or use the pot.

When we started to keep little angel "3" in Febuary 2014 "with some reservation ", because two little angels were a hand full. Since she was over a year old, couldn't walk, still couldn't talk, or use the pot. She had the same angel eye's as the other two (her eye's had that same magic). I didn't have a chance, another spell casted.

When little angel "3" first saw me, she stood back (took a long look), then moved closer to me, and then she jump in my lap. Hooked for the 3rd time, but I love it.

Although little angel "3" had won our hearts, she still needed to learn now to talk, and use the pot. She was going on two years old,

almost a year behind. The other two little angels could do all of that before then. So, little angel "3" had alot of catching up to do.

This little angel "3" was still not using the pot, and acting like she didn't know what it was for. My wife would put her on the pot, she would sit there all day 'sometimes', before she use it. I said, "how can you teach some1 how to use the pot, when they just sit there, if they have to use it or not". This seems like someone who is lazy to me. So, I said, "let me pottie train her". You shouldn't have to sit her on the pot, she should know when she has to use the pot.

The first time she didn't, I show her the pot, I spanked her hip 1 time "to get her attention", 1 more time "too let her know what she did was wrong" and a 3rd time 'to ' make sure she understood (stop after that) anymore would be abuse. I don't believe in hitting kids but sometimes you have to spank them (too make them understand).

Little angel "3" started using the pot, after that. She started going getting it, pulling her pants down, and using it on her own. She may have had a little help, from angel "1". They spent most of the year of 2015 with us.

Now, monnie and dad-dad was no longer together. Monnie had just got married to someone else. Little angel "1" didn't like this someone else. When I ask her why? She said "he act like he's good but he's not" this coming from a three year old. How wise of a statement, is that? Very, very wise, even for a grown-up. So, it wasn't that she didn't like him, something wasn't right about him. He want to move somewhere else, take them away, and monnie was planing to do this.

So, when my wife said, "it might be the last summer we see them" my heart almost stop beating. I had to sit down. I couldn't catch my breath. I felt like I was going into shock (I almost past out). Then, after over coming the shock, I ask "what do you mean not seeing them again?". She said "their mother were taking them away", the only thing that came to my mind was, "over my dead body".

I knew the only rights I had was love, but I loved them enough, to give up my freedom, and my life (too protect them). I knew little angel "1" my first little angel (my heart) didn't want to go.

I made a decision, I was willing to kill to make sure this didn't happen. So, I had a talk with "God", he already knew what I was willing

to do, because he knows everything. I ask him, "if he made this go away, I would be there for them, the rest of my life". Guest what? God did make this go away, and I must keep my promise to him. They are now stuck with me the rest of my life, 'after that' I will be watching over them (for the rest of their lifes).

However, God didn't let me know about 'it', until the end of the summer. I spent the whole summer thinking it would be my last summer with them. Every second was special, I would watch them run up and down the hill in the back yard, for hours. I wanted to record in my mind, thier faces, their laugh's, and their happiness 'forevery'.

I told my wife this book, I said "is for our memiors, if they go away, they will forget us". The though of that was almost to much for me to stand, 'so' I had to do something, to make sure that didn't happen.

Because I knew it could happen, I once kept two little girls, they forgot me (along time ago). I want these "3" little angels to always remember me, 'so' that's why I'm leaving them something, to remember me by (this book).

It was the summer of 2015, that God tested my promise to him.

God kept me in the dark (all summer long), he wanted me know (what it felt like), to lost someone you loved, so, he showed me by the though of him taken them away. Sometimes we have to lose something, too know how much it means (to us). After making this go away, God called on me, to keep my promise (right away).

He made me the "3" little angels driver to and from school, 'the rest' of the 2015 to 2016 school year. We had to get two little angels up at 6:30 each morning, that didn't want to get up, and I had to drive them to school. Each morning it was the same thing, it's to hot, turn down the radio, let down the window, speed up, and then both go to sleep. When they get to school, I had to wake them up, everymorning, and take them to their classes against their will.

The first day I took these two little angels to school (it was like) I was taking them to be hung. I had to almost drag them too the school door, and then, 'force them' to go in. Little angel "3" wasn't going to school with then, she was staying with her, "Monnie" that's what all "3" call their mother.

When I came to pick them up each day, I had to have something to drink, and a little snack. That's the first thing they looked for when they got

in the car. Then it was telling me how to drive, after all they were riding in a 300, with bucket seats, arm rest in the middle, and a sun roof top.

They were riding in style, with their own driver, telling him where they want to go, McDonald's, or too the park. I never dreamed, when I was 66, I would be two little angel's driver. But I wouldn't change it for all the money "Donald Trump" claim's he has.

After the school year was over, These "3" little angels had the best of, two worlds. They all "3" were now together. Little angel "3" was back with us for the summer, of 2016.

They would spent 1 week with us, the other week with their, "Nanna" that's what they called their greatgrandmother, her name was "Lou". Now I know the meaning of, "it takes a village to raise a child". These "3" little angels had a village, of support, and everyone had a hand in the game. God made sure his little "3" angels were well looked after. He knew, I would always keep my promise (to him) for them.

During the time away little angel "3" re-verted back to some bad habits, like not using the pot. I had to remind her, of what would happen, 'if' she fell to do this. After that, not only did she start using the pot, 'but' start going to the stool (on her own). All little angel "3" need was (to be pointed in the right directions), she can find her way (after that). Because, little angel "3" wil be that person who say, "if mess with angels 1-2, you mess with me".

I never seem "3" little girls that loved their, "Monnie" better known as "Vicky", as much as they did. That let me know, she was the right mother for them. God don't make mistakes, when it come's to his, "3 little angels", that have now (come together).

X. _Three little angels, coming together._

❧✦❧

TODAY IS SEPTEMBER 5, 2017 the first day of school for little angel "3", the 2nd year for little angels "1", and "2", (the ride to school) the first day school 'was fun'. Everyone was excited about the start, of a new school year.

When I pick the "3" little angels up from school the first day, little angel "2" was pick-up first, she was all smiles (she had a good first day), little angel "1" was pick-up next. Their classrooms were no longer next to each other. They wouldn't be able to seeing each other all day (never day) now.

Little angel "1" classroom was down the block, from little angel "2". Little angel "3" was in a different location down the street, at a church. The first day for her was kind of shocking, she had to take school shots.

She was pick-up last from school, the shock of the first day, cause her not to eat. When we picked her up, she was so hungry, she was eating cream off paper, and the paper to. Little angel "3" first day wasn't so good. School wasn't the fun she though it would be.

But to help look over them even more, "God" made it possible for

their big brother, "Cardae" to be going too the same school, that year. He was (9) years old at the time, I saw some real talent in him to, a football player. I was once a running back at Jackson State, I saw the same ability in him. So, I decided to become his mentor 'also' and help him become the football player, I could have been.

The second day of school, I though little angel "3" would not want to go, after the first day. She was all smile's the whole ride there, when I took her to the church, and smiling when I left.

Little angel "2" kinder started to cry, she wasn't use to being separated form little angel "1", they were in different parts of the school. Once I took her to the classroom, seeing her new classmates, she was alright (after that).

Little angel "1", I had to control her, she wanted to go too the classroom all on her own. I had to meet her teacher, and sign her in. This little angel would probably be teaching the class before the end of the year.

The ride home that even was nice, all "3" little angels seemed to have had a good day. They were all smile's, even little angel "2". She now knew (she had to find her place), she could no longer follow in little angel "1" shallow's. Now little angel "2", had to create her own shallow.

The next morning, little angel "1" left with some angry, little angel "3" was all smiles, and little angel "2" was still feeling somewhat alone. When we got to school, the other (2) little angels, was dropped off first, little angel "2" begin to cry. When I explain to her, "that the other (2) little angels were going to their classrooms, she was going too her classroom to", she was fine after that.

The ride home after school, everyone was somewhat quite, there wasn't anything special about that day, at school. When the (3) little angels got home, their Monnie had purchase them some new shoes, and boots that light up. This change all of their moods, soon they were running around, lighting up the house.

Every night before these (3) light angels would go to sleep, they had to have their warm milk. If I sometimes forget, they would say, "Donnie where is our warm milk, you know we can't sleep, without our warm milk". So, I had to get their warm milk. Then, maybe they would go to sleep, after being told a couple of times "to stop talking and go too

sleep". But, before little angel "1" goes to sleep every night, she always come, and give me a big hug. Sometimes it's so tight, like she didn't want to let go.

The next morning, little angel "1" came looking for me to put her new boot's that light-up, on. I was down star's, she came down and I put her new boot's, on. She then, ran back up stairs, 'so' the other two little angels could see, little angel "2" wanted her boots to light-up, and little angel "3" want shoes' that light-up.

When we left for school that morning, there were a lot of mix feelings. Everyone was quite and looking sad, except little angel "1", she had her boots on that light-up. I think she was dressing for some one special.

Little angel "2" broke the silents, by saying "Donny can we stop by McDonald, when you pick us up", I said "I'll get you some happy-meals", everyone began to smile by the mention of, "happy-meals".

Little angel "3" who had been happy the days before, was now sad over shoes that didn't light-up, something she wouldn't have notice, a couple of months ago. Her mind was now like that of a flame (that had been lit), she can now see everything. This little angel made up for a year, in just a couple of months.

The ride home that day after school, all "3" little angels were happy. They knew we were going to McDonald's for happy-meals. They were lauding and talking the whole trip, about who did this, what somebody said, and knotting someone out. This was the end to a great week at school for all (3) little angels.

The weekend, they spent with their "Nannie", she live next to the apartment, the little angels will be moving in soon. This made me very happy, this was the apartment it all begin, (5) years ago. This is where my heart was changed, same address, and same apartment.

The little angels were very excited to see their new apartment, although little angel "1" had live their before, when she was just (2) months old. This is where it begin, when she first looked into my eyes, and change my life.

God had a (5) year plan for his "3" little angels, to make sure I didn't interfere, he put me in a position that would last for (5) years, 'after

that' my blessing would be granted. He tied my make hands and feet, to make sure I stood still.

When God use you as part of his plan, you will be blessed. Because, "God" has plans for these "3" little angels, and I "thank him", for using me. They have given my life more meaning than anything else in life could ever do.

When the little "3" angels returned from the weekend, after seeing their new apartment, they were very excited, 'but' the call of our backyard was much to strong.

Soon they were running and playing in the backyard, the though of their new apartment, had vanished. They loved being outside, this was the prefect backyard for them, it was in closed, 'by' a wooden fence that surround it. So, they had their own private backyard playground.

The start of school the next week, my wife pitch in, first she needed to find out the routine of dropping them off, and picking them up. The "3" little angels were very excited leaving that morning, they would be able to boss her, like they boss (me).

My wife, "Rutha Mae Hall' who they call, "Mae" picked them up after school, they though it would be me. She took the "3" little angels shopping after school, and got their favor treat (sugar pops). When they arrived home, everyone was happy, even my wife. She loved taking them to school, picking them up, even 'if' she didn't know it at the time.

The ride home must have been special, for little angel "3", now she was making her voice heard all even. This little angel had found her 'voice', not that of a baby, 'but' as a member of the crew. She will now make her voice heard, among the other (2) little angels.

The next morning little angel "1" had a fever, was couching, and had to miss school that day. When we got to school, little angel "2" started to cry, even though her monnie, little angel "3", and big brother was there. She missed little angel "1", the source of her shallow. Little angel "2" hadn't found her own shallow (yet).

When I returning home, little angel "1" was all smiles, he had me all to herself. After hanging on my leg for about 30 minutes, the cold started coming out her noise. She felt must better after that, I guest we were a cure for each other.

I didn't know how little angel "2" day went, sense she was crying

when I drop her off for school. I got my answer the second I walk in her classroom, (when she saw me) her whole face lit up. She ran to me grabbing both of my legs.

She didn't even ask about little angel "1", she was just happy to see me. Little angel "1" had went with my wife to take their "Ganna", to the doctor. The ride home was very happy, little angel "1" wasn't even missed.

The next morning it was raining, and the sky's were cloudy, "but" the "3" little angels were all smiles. This made it seem like a bright sunny day, little angel "3" was happy she had shoes that light-up, little angel "2" was glad her shallow was back, and little angel "1" was glad to go back too school. Things became even brighter, with the promise of McDonald's "happy-meals", after school.

I think little angel "1" learned something the day she miss school sick. She found out, that I would be there when she came from school (she wouldn't miss anything), 'but if' she missed school, she could miss a lot. I said she a was very smart (little angel "1").

After school that day, with the excitement of, "happy-meals" we almost forgot little angel "3". I had passed her pick-up a block, I had to turn around too come back, and get her. When I picked her up, she had a treat, and didn't want to share it with the other "2" little angels. So, I don't think little angel "3" cared about us being late.

The next morning little angel "1" left for school with angry, she didn't like the uniform, she was wearing. She wanted to wear a dress with her boots, that she wore the day before.

The uniform she wore today was pants and shoes, this never was a problem before. I think it's a boy. When we reached school, the crossing guard said, "she look a little sad today", I said "she wanted to wear a dress, I think she have a boyfriend" little angel "1" quickly replied, "no I don't!!", that mean's she do.

On the way home from school that even, everyone was very quite, then a song came on the radio. It was the Temptation, singing "My girl", little angel "1" said, "turn it up", I said, "what do you know about that", all "3" little angels starting singing in harmony. The rest of the ride home, was a joy ride.

The next morning, the last day for the week, all "3" little angels

were especially happy. Not because it was the last day, 'but' their dad-dad was picking them up after school. He was working out of town. He came back to help them move to their new apartment, that was next door to where he was staying, "6610 south Peoria" on the 3rd floor. The same apartment we had lived (5) years ago before moving to "9304 south Vanderpoel".

Just like it was (5) years ago, when we stayed at "6608 south Peoria" on the same floor, it took (30) years for me to complete the circle. Little angel "1" had completed it in just (5) years, "God" have other plans for his "3" little angels, and it all starts now. I will always be thankfully that he use me, to help carry out those plans.

Now that all "3" little angels are back at the place, that God blessed me from, 'by' bringing them into my life, I know their true blessings are yet to come.

XI. *Where it all begin "6608 south Peoria", 3rd floor.*

❦

ON OCTOBER *1, 2017,* all "3" little angels moved to the place, little angel "1" change my heart, (5) years ago. The place where "God" blessed me for the third time, the first time was with a son "Tony", the second time was a daughter "Poopy", and the third time with these, "3" little angels. God blessed us (3) times to let us know it was him.

Now little angel "1" in back to the place it all begin. Back at 6608 south Peoria, on the 3rd floor, in the same apartment we lived-in, when she change my heart. This little angel have become full circled in just (5) years, meaning little angel "1" have a lot more circles to complete. It took me (30) years to complete my circle.

My circle was for a job career, that took (30) years to complete. Little angel "1" circle was her childhood career, that took (5) years to complete, "God" is ready to work with her now, and she is ready for is task.

We both became full circled, at the same address "6608 south Peoria", the same apartment, on the 3rd floor, a sign from, "God". He let us know, it was him.

Completing one's circle don't mean death, 'it' means you have other circles to complete. This is a goal most people never reach, little angel "1" reach it in (5) years, and that's very special. God has greater goals in the future for her (as well) as little angel "2", and little angel "3". All (3) were sent from, "God".

Some people think a blessing is, when they get a promotion on your job, "no" you earn it, some think when they win money, 'no' you got lucky. A blessing is something you had nothing to do with, 'no' knowledge of, 'no' control of, and 'no' say in.

These "3" little angels, I had 'no' say, control, or anything to do with (God put them in my life). Now he's letting me know, I'm during things right.

God brought them threw the same path as he brought us, we live in the same apartment (5) years ago (little angel "1" is 5 years old), back in the same apartment in (5) years, and my plan's are for all "3" little angels to move back to their real home in (5) years (9304 south Vanderpoel). My lucky number was #3, these "3" little angels lucky number, is the #5.

So, in (5) years, 'if' my plans are "Gods" plans, the "3" little angels will be moving back to (9304 south Vanderpoel). Only this time it will belong to them. Because in (5) years my plans will be, (to move) too a warmer place.

Since God is during the driving, I will wait those (5) years, for him to show me the place, just like he did before, at 9304 south Vanderpoel. A place for his "3" little angels to grow-up. Then another special place on earth, (for me) as in heaven.

God's first blessing for his (3) little angels were their new apartment with a beautiful wooden bunk bed, They were so happy when they saw it, it had star's "so" they could climb to the top bunk. All (3) loved to climb, God knew this, since he knows everything.

Because I found out, along time ago, "God" was directing my life. I was just a silent rider, he was during all the driving. Now he's directing my little "3" angels the same way, he directed me. I summit to him, and he allow me "to" be me.

Now these "3" little angels were a blessing to us. We had nothing to do with, no control, and say "God did". He put them into our lives,

because we knew how much we would love them. Our love is so strong, we would come back from the dead, "if" they need us, "so" nowhere on this earth, we wouldn't go for them "or" nothing on earth, we wouldn't do for them.

I know our "3" little angels will achieve their goals, because they have the power of #3 pulling for them. (1) The power of God. (2) The power of them. (3) The power of us. As long as God keep our eyes open, they can always count on us. The #3 indicates his answer.

I remember one Thanksgiving eve the (3) little angels were drawing pictures in the basement, they would run from the basement to the 2nd floor to show "Mae " their drawings, they wanted to impress her. These (3) little angels made all our holidays, and every day a joy.

That night I had a bad dream about little angel "1", I dream she didn't want to be with me (I woke up in shock), it was just 5am (I had to get up). I went down stars to make coffee, then I heard someone coming down stars (I though it was my wife) 'but' it was little angel "1" (God had woke her up at 5am) to let me know it was only a dream.

To show you God like's a good joke, after Thanksgiving diner, and a bath the (2) other little angels took a nap. Not little angel "1", she now had me all to herself "so' I had to watch "Mickey Mouse" instead of football. I love little angel "1" with all my heart (still I wanted to watch football).

The day after Thanksgiving the (3) little angels wanted to help me get the leaves in the backyard up, I made a pile for them to play, after playing in the leaves (little angels "2-3' became tired of the leaves, and started playing with something else. I was cleaning the back part of the yard, when I return little angel "1" had picked up most of the leaves (5 bags), I guest she was making up for making me watch "Mickey Mouse" on Thanksgiving day (instead of football).

The next day a Saturday, it was to cold for the little angels to go outside 'so' they use their indoor playground (the basement). All day long they were running and placing orders. Donnie!, "I want grits, cereals, after that, 'go' get us a Happy Meal, then more cereals, after that they wanted me to cook them an egg, then salad, after that strawberries with each little angel wanted something different on their strawberries, angel "1" wanted sour cream, angel "2" wanted whip cream, and angel

"3" wanted salt. They ran me all day long with their orders 'but' I wouldn't change it for all the money in the world.

That Sunday morning my wife and the (3) little angels got dress for Sun-day school, and church. If you are wondering did I go? The answer is, "no", I said before, "I have a direct line to God". However I do believe in people going to church, it teaches people that may not know God (about God).

I know God (I still don't go to church), the reason I don't go (I see the people that do), I know God can't be present there. Man have long ago driven God from the church (trying to play him). The people in the church can't hear the message from God (trying to speck for him). When you truly know God his message for you will be clear, and your future will be revealed. I now know what my future looks like (from nowhere to paradise).

The weeks leading up to X-mas the little angels were back home going to school staying with us on the week-end. We had put up a X-mas tree without any presents under it, little angel "1" notice this.

Their mother was in the process of moving during this time, she said "it may not be a X-mas this year, little angel "1" said "what are we going to do, you don't having nothing, Mannia don't have nothing, Mae and Donny don't have nothing' but ' I did over hear them talking about getting us something"

So when we picked them up the Friday before X-mas they looked kinder down. They hadn't saw any presents under the tree when they left 'so' there was no reason to think any presents would be there now.

When they walk in the door and saw all the presents under the tree, their faces lit up the whole room, they now couldn't wait to X-mas. It was 3 days to X-mas, everyday they ask how long before X-mas, they now couldn't wait till X-mas came.

That Sunday my wife took them to church for a X-mas service, afterwards they were given candy and gifts this took the excitement 'off' of what was under the X-mas tree for a day.

The next day was Monday X-mas eve, my daughter "Poopy" always have a diner for the mothers, the excitement of the even cause all 3 little angels to go to sleep before 7pm, something they had never done before 'or' maybe it was all the waiting for X-mas that did it.

This gave me a chance to put together a stove my wife brought for them for X-mas. Something I though I could do in a couple of hours. When I started taking parts out of the box, I knew it maybe an all night-er, I was right. There was all these parts, screws, and little or no direction on what goes where. It was trail and error until early morning I got it all put together. During this time my wife looked down stairs saw all the parts and went back up stairs, saying "if you need me call me" that's the last I heard from her that night.

After that I was finally able to get a couple hours of sleep, they had slept the whole night all the waiting for X-mas had wore them down. That morning when I woke them up saying "Merry X-mas" they almost ran over me trying to get down stairs. I had to make them go back up stairs, wash their faces, and brush their teeth.

When they came back down stairs there where no presents under the tree, all 3 said at the same time "where are the presents"? I said "check the basement they maybe there". When they saw the stove (I had spent most of the night putting together) all the other presents, the joy on their faces made it all worth it. That X-mas they got presents from everyone, uncles, cousins, and friends. Just like Jesus received many presents on the day of his birth, God did the same for his little angels on the day of his birth.

The next day was December 26, 2018 my birthday, making me 69 years young. God had just given me the greatest birthday present of all (he allowed our little angels to spend X-mas with us). Now they were going to their Mannia for a new round of present openings, God is blessing his little angels (like he has bless us).

Since God has given me so many blessings (you may say why shouldn't I go to church to thank him)? If it's God's will (then I will have to go), his will shall be done. Because his will comes with the power of "God" no man can resist.

He knows our minds 'so' God has blessed me with so many blessings for the one thing I though he took from me (my brother). I was angry at God for many, many years for that (he knew this) that's why God gave me many, many more brothers as replacements. You can't keep anything form God (he knows your mind) 'so' he did this until I was able to see.

God took my brother and gave me many, many brothers (then he

saw I had no sisters) now many, many women call me "brother". He makes our life's many, many times better (when we though it was bad).

There once was a person who call me brother (who had a twin brother) "Freddie & Eddie Hannah" although he loved his twin brother (he prefer me over him), he had been with his twin brother all their lives (this hurtled his twin brother), but still his twin brother called me "brother".

My wife and I, use to wonder why God didn't allow us to have children. Now we think (we know). He had special children for us planed. My son "Tony", my daughter "Poopy", and "3 little angels", the number (3) again. Now we truly know this is "God's plan" full-filled. The lest of 'us' become the best of 'us' (my life story is a prefect example of that).

One day my wife ask me, "why do you keep calling them angels?", I said "because they are, God sent". When people think of angels (they think of someone with wings) 'but' some angels you can't see (the one's with wings), and some angels you can see (they were created at birth), same as Jesus.

I once knew a lady that had (3) daughters (she didn't teach them to love one-another) instead she allowed them to hate each other. After her death, the oldest daughter said, "I no longer have any sisters", God heard her statement (he took both of her sisters). Now she have no sisters.

You see, fruit don't fall far from the tree, 'if" the tree is baring the fruits of God, then the fruits that fall, will be (Godly fruit).

Because God is a (forgiving God), he forgave her for all the wrongs, and bad things she had done (like forcing him to take her sisters). To show his forgiveness (God gave her 2 daughters). Now it's up to her to decide 'if" she has something worth living 'or' dying for, 'by' teaching them the things her mother didn't teach her (love instead of hate).

A great man once said, "if you don't have something you're willing to die for, you'r already dead". Now we have (3) somethings, we're willing to die for. God have made us the richest people alive (because we wouldn't trade our live's for all the richest in the world). What we have, money can't buy (blessings from God).

The End.

A tribute to my wife, "Rutha M. Hall"